K'VOD HAMET
A GUIDE FOR THE BEREAVED

Rabbi Stuart Kelman

EKS Publishing Co., Albany, California

Project Editor
Jessica W. Goldstein

Book Design
Irene Imfeld

K'vod HaMet: A Guide for the Bereaved, Third Edition, © 2002 by EKS Publishing Co. Printed in Canada. No part of this book may be transmitted or reproduced by any means, electronic or mechanical, without written permission, except for brief quotations included in critical articles and reviews. For information contact the publisher.

First Edition December 1992

Second Edition September 1995. The second edition was underwritten by Helen and Sandy Schneider in loving memory of Rose and Leon Schneider and Sophie and Max Slavin.

This third edition was underwritten by Mrs. Esther Kelman, in loving memory of Wilson Kelman and Patti Beth Kelman Mintz. May their memories be for a blessing.

EKS Publishing Co.
P.O. Box 9750
Berkeley, California 94709-0750

email: orders@ekspublishing.com
Phone (510) 558-9200, Fax (510) 558-9255
www.ekspublishing.com

First Printing, October 2002

ISBN 0-939144-41-7

Then Job arose, tore his robe, cut off his hair,
and threw himself on the ground and worshipped.
He said, "Naked came I out of my mothers womb,
and naked shall I return there; Adonai has given
and Adonai has taken away;
blessed be the name of Adonai.

Job 1:21

A season is set for everything,
a time for every experience under heaven:
A time for being born and a time for dying,
A time for planting and a time for uprooting the planted;
A time for slaying and a time for healing,
A time for tearing down and time for building up;
A time for weeping and a time for laughing;
A time for wailing and a time for dancing . . .

Kohelet 3:1-4

Contents

Foreword 7

PART I: JEWISH TRADITIONS FOR DEATH AND MOURNING

Chapter 1 The Basics 10
Chapter 2 Burial and Funeral Preparations 15
Chapter 3 The Funeral and Burial Service 21
Chapter 4 *Shivah*: The Healing Begins 27
Chapter 5 *Sh'loshim* and Beyond:
           Attaining Acceptance 33
Chapter 6 Guidelines for Grieving 39
Chapter 7 Checklist of Important Information 43

PART II: COMPENDIUM OF PRAYERS

Chapter 8 Selection of Prayers
           Mourners' *Kaddish*
               (to be recited with a *minyan*) 46
           Kaddish at a Burial
               (to be recited with a *minyan*) 48
           Al Malei Rachamim
               (may be recited individually) 50
           Lighting the *Shiva* Candle (two options) .. 52
           Conclusion of *Shiva* 54
           Lighting a *Yahrzeit* Candle 56
Chapter 9 Service for an Unveiling of a Marker 58

Appendix 1 Glossary of Hebrew Terms 67
Appendix 2 Notes 69
Appendix 3 Bibliography and Suggestions
            for Further Reading 70

Foreword

This handbook was originally published as part of the United Jewish Appeal Leadership Cabinet Judaica Series. It was written by Rabbi Daniel Pressman of Congregation Beth David in Saratoga, California, and Rabbi Frederic Margulies of Wilmette, Illinois, under the guidance of series editor Naomi Patz. Second editions of the work were prepared by Rabbi Marvin Goodman of Foster City, California, and Rabbi Gordon Freeman of Walnut Creek, California. I prepared this third edition based on the work of my colleagues and my own experiences as a mourner, friend, and rabbi.

This pamphlet is about death, an unpleasant subject and an unpredictable event. When someone dies, the fabric of life is torn, and most people find it very difficult to make decisions regarding appropriate funeral arrangements. Thankfully, *halachah* and the experience of Jews throughout the generations comes to our aid and helps simplify the decision-making process.

This booklet is written from a Conservative perspective. It is important to realize that Conservative Judaism has largely retained the traditional practices of Jewish law. It is discouraging to see a Jew omit a particular practice because it is thought to be "Orthodox," without first weighing and evaluating that practice's benefits. We believe that Jewish burial and mourning practices are so wise, comforting, and psychologically sound that we can all benefit from them, regardless of where we place ourselves on the religious spectrum.

Our congregation, Netivot Shalom in Berkeley, California, has organized a *Chevra Kadisha* (Holy Society) that helps the bereaved when a family member dies. The Holy Society is made up of the following four committees:

1. *Taharah*—The *Taharah* committee performs the ritual for preparing a body for burial, a ritual that includes washing the body and dressing the deceased in shrouds.
2. *Sh'mirah*—Members of the *sh'mirah* committee are responsible for watching over or guarding the body, which has been draped or laid to rest in a closed casket, before the funeral.
3. *Gemilut Chasadim*—This group offers support services for the mourner and his or her family after a death. Members of the *gemilut chasadim* committee may cook for the family, drive car-pools, or perform other helpful tasks.
4. *Nechamah*—Members of the *nechamah* group provide grief counseling and help mourners understand the laws concerning death and mourning. At Netivot Shalom, we assign one committee member to be with a mourner for a full year. These counselors offer a sympathetic ear and have access to support materials (such as pamphlets that give parents advice on explaining death to children) that may help people as they progress through the stages of mourning.

The collective efforts of the *Chevra Kadisha* create a wonderfully caring community. I hope that you will read this pamphlet carefully. It is written for those who have suffered a loss as well as for the friends of these mourners. After reading this pamphlet, you should discuss its contents with your family and bring questions that arise to members of your synagogue's *Chevra Kadisha*. In doing so, you will be better prepared to face mourning yourself or comfort others in their own grief.

Rabbi Stuart Kelman
Congregation Netivot Shalom
Berkeley, CA
5763

Part I

Jewish Traditions for Death and Mourning

Chapter 1
The Basics

THE MOURNERS

Traditionally, one observes the laws of mourning upon the death of a father, mother, brother, sister, son, daughter, or spouse. It is for these seven relationships that Jewish mourning customs and laws, including sitting *Shivah*, saying *Kaddish*, observing *Yahrzeit*, apply.

You may also wish to formally mourn the loss of someone outside these seven relationships. If you are grieving for a grandparent, stepparent, in-law, or close friend, you should seek out appropriate mourning rituals. Some rabbis advise that you follow the traditional practices for these relations, while others recommend a modified mourning. Your rabbi can help you to determine the most appropriate course of mourning in these cases.

Because the human emotional response to death is so complex, the Jewish laws of mourning take into account many different aspects of grief. However, two guiding precepts or threads run through all Jewish rituals related to death and mourning, namely *k'vod hamet* (respect for the dead) and *nichum aveilim* (consoling the mourners).

K'vod hamet means that the body of the deceased person deserves respect and care. The human body is not just a lump of lifeless matter to be treated casually or callously. In fact, its condition may be compared to a *Sefer Torah* (Torah scroll) that has become *pasul* (unusable). Because that scroll was holy and still contains holy words, it must be treated with reverence, even after its physical structure has been damaged. We therefore bury—never burn or toss away—old Torah scrolls. Similarly, the human body houses a holy spark and is a reflection of the *pasul* (the image of God). Because the body retains its holiness even after death, we must take care to treat it with respect. The funeral rituals we are about to discuss reflect many aspects of this principle.

Nichum aveilim is the act of consoling the mourners. When we comfort mourners, we bring into this world some of the healing and harmony of the World to Come. This *mitzvah* assumes that mourners should not be alone in their grief and that it is the duty of a mourner's friends, family, and community to provide support to the grieving. Some of the rituals of mourning are designed to bring people together for support, while others exist to help mourners acknowledge and accept the reality of death.

WHAT DO I DO WHEN SOMEONE DIES?

Let's assume that someone close to you has died. If the responsibility for arranging the funeral falls to you, you need to reach out in two directions: to the mortuary, which will make the physical arrangements for burial, and to the religious community, which will give you support and counsel. It is common practice to first contact the congregation's president, vice president, or *Chevra Kadisha* coordinator and the rabbi. These people will help you make the funeral arrangements and some important decisions. The time for the funeral generally needs to be set with the rabbi. You also must contact the mortuary and, in some cases, the cemetery as well. In some communities, the *Chevra Kadisha* will contact the funeral home on behalf of the family. You should consider contacting your congregation any time there is a death in your family, even if you will not be responsible for funeral arrangements or if the funeral will be held out of town. Other congregants will still be able to offer you emotional support and can help you with whatever practical arrangements are your responsibility.

You may have questions concerning whom to notify about a funeral. Perhaps some members of your family are estranged from you, the deceased, or one another. I urge you to consider this time as an ideal opportunity to heal any breach. Every mourner has the right to be notified of a family member's death and to participate in all mourning rituals. It is even possible that death will cast a new light on old grievances and may help bring about reconciliation.

The time between someone's death and the funeral is called *aninut*, and before the funeral the bereaved family member is called an *onayn*. During this period of intense shock and grief, the survivors are relieved of almost all social and ritual obligations outside of making burial and funeral preparations. The bereaved are relieved of their normal duties and responsibilities for two reasons: First, in accordance with the principle of *k'vod hamet*, the *mitzvah* of attending to the deceased must take precedence over all other grieving. Second, Jewish law recognizes that people feel pulled out of regular life when someone close to them dies and wisely focuses the mourner's attention on the needs of the deceased. Audrey Gordon, a respected death educator, writes:

> Making funeral plans serves as a necessary activity for the mourner at the beginning of the grief process. The mourner reaffirms concern for the dead through actions, which serve at the same time to overcome the wish for identification, and incorporation with the lost loved one. The *onayn*, through actions, experiences the fact that he or she is "not dead," not still and lifeless, as one may consciously or unconsciously feel or wish to be. During this first period of grief there is an intense desire on the part of the bereaved to do whatever possible for the departed. Jewish tradition meets this need by placing the responsibility for all the funeral arrangements on the mourners, not by shielding and excusing them from these tasks.[1]

The bereaved should not, however, be left alone to make these decisions. In the first hours after a death, immediate family members are not likely to be thinking clearly, and funeral arrangements involve a significant outlay of money. Mourners should seek guidance from their rabbi, members of the *Chevra Kadisha*, and friends and family.

For friends of the mourner, the period of *aninut* is a particularly delicate time. *Pirkei Avot* advises "Do not try to comfort (your friend) while one's dead lies before him or her" (4:18). This means that a silent hug or a helping gesture are worth far more than words at this time of peak stress. Although friends should not, under normal circumstances, completely take over the funeral arrangements, they can help in many other ways: driving or accompanying the mourner as he or she makes the arrangements, taking care of the mourner's children, or picking up incoming family at the airport. Above all, offer your support. Don't feel that you are obligated to come up with the one magic phrase that will make everything right again. No such words exist. But your presence and your concern are of great value. Certain laws and customs pertain to preparations for burial and it is important to be aware of them. These customs are described in the following pages.

Chapter 2
Burial and Funeral Preparations

MAKING THE ARRANGEMENTS

Certain decisions have to be made almost immediately: The mourner must choose a mortuary, set the time for the funeral, make arrangements for a cemetery plot, select a casket, and notify family and friends. The first step should be determining if any arrangements have already been made (i.e. if the deceased purchased a burial plot).

TIMELY BURIAL

According to Jewish law, the deceased should be buried as soon as is possible, preferably within twenty-four hours of death. This is another aspect of *k'vod hamet*, since leaving the corpse unburied was considered to be a humiliation of the dead.[2] Prompt burial has psychological benefits, too. The funeral, the act of burial, and the first recitation of *Kaddish*, which takes place by the grave, are of great value in beginning the mourning process. Long delays between death and burial put a great deal of strain on the mourners, leaving them in an emotional limbo. Every effort should be made to expedite the funeral. Delays are permitted in order to honor the dead. For example: we may wait for a proper casket to be delivered, for close relatives to arrive from out of town, or for legal reasons (such as a coroner-mandated autopsy). Even in the latter case, there may be ways to avoid undue delay, and your rabbi is prepared to intervene in certain circumstances. We do not bury on Shabbat or during many holidays. Different synagogues have different rules concerning when burial is permitted, so you should consult your rabbi if a family member dies on or near a holiday.

TAHARAH: PREPARING THE BODY FOR BURIAL

Jewish tradition calls for the entire body to be returned to the earth and prohibits embalming. The body is allowed to decompose in a natural way and to thereby fulfill the edict that "For dust you are, and to dust you shall return" (Gen. 3:19). Furthermore, embalming inevitably involves invasive procedures that violate the integrity of the body and treat it disrespectfully; the body is not an object to be manipulated. Respect for the integrity of the body is one reason behind the Jewish objection to viewing the body, as cosmetic procedures can also be disrespectful to the remains of the deceased. In some rare situations, civil law requires a body be embalmed. But even then, exceptions or alternatives often can be arranged. The rabbi and the funeral director can help to you in such cases. Jewish law prescribes a special ritual to prepare the body for burial called *Taharah* (purification). "Just as a newborn child is immediately washed and enters this world clean and pure, so he who departs this world must be cleansed and made pure through the religious ritual called *Taharah*."[3] This ritual consists of washing the body, an act performed by members of the

Chevra Kadisha. A special booklet detailing these rituals, *Chesed Shel Emet*, can be obtained from EKS Publishing Company (see bibliography).

Judaism has a lovely and meaningful tradition of dressing the dead in simple white garments, called *tachrichim*. The practice of being buried in *tachrichim* underscores the equality of all people—a condition most obvious at the time of death—and reflects the Jewish sensibility that funerals should be kept simple and avoid any displays of wealth. The use of white linen shrouds also recalls the garment worn by the high priest on Yom Kippur, when he would enter the Holy of Holies of the Temple to ask forgiveness for his sins and the sins of the Jewish people. By analogy, when facing one's Maker, a person should be humble and contrite, wearing simple, white, unadorned linen garments. Many traditional Jews underscore the connection between judgment and death by wearing white, shroud-like garments annually on Yom Kippur.

SH'MIRAH: WATCHING/GUARDING

We demonstrate regard for the deceased by treating the body with respect, beginning at the moment of death. According to *halachah* (Jewish law), the body should not be left alone. Jewish funerals are understood in part as a *l'vayah*, or accompanying, of the body to the grave. Traditional Jews and *Chevra Kadisha*s observe this law by having a *shomer*, or guardian, be with the deceased at all times. Usually the *shomer* reads from the Book of Job, Psalms, or other writings on the subject of death while sitting with the body. Congregations often maintain a library of suggested reading material. Friends, grandchildren, and members of the deceased person's extended family may choose to be *shomrim*. Communities differ on when *sh'mirah* begins; some begin at the time of death, while others wait until *Taharah* has been completed (Communities also differ on the time *Taharah* is performed). Consult your rabbi for the custom of your community.

AUTOPSY AND ORGAN DONATION

Given the Jewish mandate to respect the dead, you may have questions about the Jewish perspective on autopsies and organ donation. To begin, we caution you that this is a complex issue. Every situation is unique, and your rabbi can help you make decisions according to your particular circumstances. However, a few general statements are appropriate. Reverance for life is an important principle in Jewish law and means that human life and health must take precedence over most other ritual commandments. Any question about an autopsy or organ donation should therefore be evaluated against the measure of possible benefit. Where a violation of *k'vod hamet* will be counterbalanced by a true benefit to human life, most rabbis will sanction the violation.

In cases where, for legal reasons, the coroner requires an autopsy, all branches of Judaism yield to the demands of the state. In the past, some coroners have been sensitive to Jewish concerns and have avoided performing or limited the scope of autopsies when other sources of information could substitute.

Organ transplants are, if anything, even more clearly related to preservation of life. Authorities in all three movements have been quite lenient in permitting organ donation. In 1999, the Rabbinical Assembly Committee on Jewish Law and Standards of the Conservative Movement ruled that one is obligated to permit postmortem transplantation of his or her organs for life-saving medical procedures and that withholding consent for such organ donation is contrary to Jewish law. As Rabbi Elliot Dorff, rector of the University of Judaism, stated: "The overriding principles of honoring the dead and saving lives work in tandem. That is, saving a person's life is so sacred a value in Judaism that if a person's organ can be used to save someone else's life, it is actually an honor to the deceased."

THE CASKET

According to Jewish tradition, a person should be buried in a plain wood *aron* (casket). Wood caskets allow for decomposition and facilitate the process of going from "dust to dust." Metal caskets interfere with this organic process and should be avoided. Jewish tradition also considers metal caskets needlessly ostentatious and expensive, qualities that contradict the simplicity and equality rabbis valued. Ideally, practical Jewish burial customs emphasize the finality and reality of death. In Audrey Gordon's words, "A funeral according to *halachah* emphasizes that death is death."[5]

VIEWING, EMBALMING, AND CREMATION

We do not open the casket during the funeral out of respect for the deceased. It is seen as creating an unequal relationship, and therefore disrespectful to look upon someone who cannot look back at you. Jewish law also forbids cremation, for three reasons. First, we want the body to return to the earth in as natural a way as possible. Nature is not the enemy, it is only the medium through which we live out our lives and deaths. Second, we do not want to rob the mourners of the experience of mourning. While some people may think that cremation prevents excessive mourning, experience has shown just the opposite. When mourners are deprived of the experience of burial or of a grave, they may be less able to complete the mourning process. Many Jews also avoid cremation in order to distance themselves from the crematoriums of World War II. For all these reasons, most rabbis will not officiate at a cremation.

Chapter 3
The Funeral and Burial Service

THE FUNERAL SERVICE

The Jewish funeral service is brief. It consists of the recitation of a Psalm or two and perhaps some other traditional texts, a eulogy, and the *El Malei Rachamim* ("O God, full of compassion") prayer. *Kaddish*, the best-known prayer related to death and mourning, is not said until after the burial.

The *hesped* (eulogy) is a very important part of the funeral. *Eulogy* means "a good word," and a good eulogy is exactly that—a few words that convey someone's personality and accomplishments, not a full biography. The eulogizer should also try to express the sense of loss experienced by the survivors. Most rabbis will spend time talking with the family, even if they were well acquainted with the deceased, to learn more about the family's relationship with that person. Such discussions not only help the rabbi to write a good, appropriate eulogy, but they also give mourners and important outlet for their emotions. Realizing that happy memories endure long after death can be a balm for mourners, and the eulogy interview can be quite therapeutic. In addition to the rabbi's eulogy, immediate family members or friends will sometimes say a few words about their loved one or read an appropriate poem or letter.

CHILDREN AND FUNERALS

People often wonder if children should be present at a funeral. There is no reason, according to tradition, for a child to be excluded. It is important to realize that children, like adults, experience loss and grief when someone dies. What's more, their relative inexperience can lead them to misinterpret the tensions and grief present in the house and conclude that they are somehow at fault. It is important for adults to take time to explain what has happened to children, to listen to children's feelings, and to dispel any incorrect conclusions they may have drawn. Earl Grollman's *Talking About Death: A Dialogue between Child and Parent* is an excellent resource for conducting such a discussion.

If you deny children the opportunity to attend a funeral, it suggests to them that their feelings don't count. Many adults remember with anger and resentment such exclusion when they were children. Through you, your children learn about grief and come to understand that death is an inevitable part of life. This lesson is not easy, but it will be better than the fantasies and imaginings that an excluded child may have.

If you have any questions about a specific child's attendance at a funeral, you should consult your rabbi. If you are the parent and a mourner, you might want to have a close friend near you to help with the children during the funeral itself, so that you won't be distracted from your own grieving. But take care not to shunt the children aside or send them away during *shivah*. We do our children no service when we "protect" them in this way. We help them when we explain what is happening and allow them to participate.

K'RIAH AND THE KADDISH

The ceremony of K'riah, or tearing the clothing, takes place before the funeral ceremony. K'riah is probably the oldest mourning ritual we have, dating back to biblical days. Some actually tear a garment (the lapel of a jacket, for example); others tear a black ribbon that has been attached to the mourner's garment. After the tearing, recite the following blessing:

בָּרוּךְ אַתָּה יְיָ אֱלוֹהֵינוּ מֶלֶךְ הָעוֹלָם דַּיַּן הָאֱמֶת.

Baruch atah Adonai Eloheinu melech ha'olam dayan ha'emet

Praised are you, Adonai our God, Ruler of the Universe, righteous Judge.

יְיָ נָתַן וַיְיָ לָקָח, יְהִי שֵׁם יְיָ מְבֹרָךְ.

Adonai natan v'Adonai lakach; y'hi sheim Adonai m'vorach.

Adonai has given and Adonai has taken; praised be the name of Adonai.

During K'riah, we acknowledge the finite nature of life. How remarkable that, at a moment of grief, we recite a blessing! Furthermore, we recite it standing up. "The posture of accepting grief in Jewish life is always upright, symbolizing both strength in the face of crisis and respect for the deceased."[6] But how can someone calmly accept the death of a loved one, and even say a blessing over it? Joel Wolowelsky explains:

While the outward display of certain emotions is not fully accepted in our society, it is well known that mourners normally experience anger as a reaction to death. There is anger towards the deceased for abandoning and "inconveniencing" them, and anger towards themselves—guilt—for feeling that anger. Similarly, there may be anger towards God for allowing this to happen, and—especially for the religious person—this reaction, too, might create feelings of guilt. The tearing of one's clothes might seem to be a spontaneous release, but the series of *halachic* requirements actually turn it into a controlled reaction. Studies have found that it is a great relief for the bereaved to have been able to express these feelings and to learn that it was neither uncommon nor uniquely wicked to have them. *K'riah* allows emotions which may border on frightening rage to be expressed as controlled, healthy anger.[7]

AT THE CEMETERY

The Hebrew word for funeral is *l'vayah* (accompanying). Originally, the procession to the cemetery was an integral part of the ceremony. Nowadays, when the funeral chapel is often quite distant from the cemetery, we have a procession of automobiles, and then, when we arrive at the cemetery, we have a real procession following the casket. The procession stops seven times on its way to the burial site, each stop expressing regret for the need of such a task.

The principal parts of the burial service are lowering the casket into the ground, reciting the *Tzidduk Ha-din* (a prayer of acceptance), replacing the earth in the grave, and reciting *Kaddish*. It is a *mitzvah* for each person to help cover the casket by shoveling earth into the grave. Furthermore, each of us is obligated to perform this *mitzvah* in its entirety. The shovel is not handed from one person to another; instead, the shovel is returned to the ground after each turn and the next person begins by withdrawing it. Often, the shovel is inverted, again a symbol of our reluctance to perform this task.

The sound of the earth striking the coffin is stark and harsh, but for many mourners this sound is often their first moment of realization that their loved one has died, and therefore the beginning of acceptance and healing. It is, in fact, the moment when the bereaved (until now an *onein*) becomes an *aveil* (a formal mourner). Some people try to avoid this very difficult moment, but it is the last act of *chesed* (loving kindness) we can perform for anyone. Judaism teaches us that anything we do to accompany the dead to his or her final burial is an act of *chesed* because it is the one thing we do for another person for which we can never be thanked or repaid. Another custom, placing some earth from Israel in the coffin, links us to the land of Israel.

After the casket is covered, mourners recite *Kaddish* for the first time. *Kaddish* does not deal directly with death, but instead speaks of the power and majesty of God. Perhaps the rabbis understood that it is at times like this, when people experience extreme grief, that they are likely to deny the existence of God. So we recite the *Kaddish* and reaffirm our belief. We also express our feelings of loss and voice the hope that God will fill the vacuum that has been created in the world. The last ritual at the cemetery has been movingly described by Deborah Lipstadt:

> One should not tarry at the cemetery for too long a period of time. The soul has been entrusted to its Maker, and all that lies in the earth is the shell that housed it during its sojourn on earth. To linger at such a time would, in most cases, accent the pain and the grief. One is loath, as I was, to hurry from the cemetery. It is unhealthy to remain too long and so hard to turn one's back and leave. It is possible that the rabbis had this emotional dilemma in mind when they created the following custom. All those present, except the immediate family, form parallel lines a few feet apart and the mourners slowly pass through. They pause a number of times as those present say:

הַמָּקוֹם יְנַחֵם (אֶתְכֶם/אוֹתְךָ/אוֹתָךְ) בְּתוֹךְ שְׁאָר אֲבֵלֵי צִיּוֹן וִירוּשָׁלָיִם.

Hamakom y'nacheim (etchem/otcha/otach) b'toch sh'ar aveilei Tziyon Virushalayim.

> *M*ay God comfort you and all who have mourned for Zion and Jerusalem.

The act of leaving the cemetery is done slowly. Even as one symbolically pauses, the period of mourning and the comforting that accompanies it begins. The community physically surrounds and envelops the mourner. Though they ask that God comfort you, their physical presence is a sign that they, too, will work to ease the pain.[8]

Chapter 4
Shivah: The Process of Healing

GRIEF

One should not grieve too much for the dead, and whoever grieves excessively is really grieving for someone else. The *Shulchan Aruch* has set limits for every stage of grief, and we may not add to them: "three [days] for weeping, seven for lamenting, and thirty for abstaining from laundered garments and from cutting the hair—and no more."[9]

Here is a profound piece of wisdom. The *Shulchan Aruch* tells us that we need to mourn and grieve, but that we also need to assimilate our loss and return to life. The post-funeral mourning periods represent a phased return to normal life, with each mourning period less intense than the previous one. The purpose of *shivah* is to begin the process of healing. It is a time to stop normal activities and reflect upon the life of the deceased and your relationship with him or her. Through remembrance, we are able to heal. Healing requires time, and so Jewish tradition prescribes a week at home, giving ourselves the time we need to mourn. However busy we may be (and we are all busy people with many commitments), it would be wise to heed our tradition and serve our emotional and psychological needs by truly "sitting" *shivah*. *Shivah* means "seven," and that does seem to be the ideal amount of time to remain at home. Why not take the time you need now while you are officially entitled to it?

AT THE HOUSE OF SHIVAH

Ideally, *shivah* should be observed by all relatives in the house of the deceased. A person's home is, after all, the place where the tangible remains of his or her life surround you, and it is only right that such reminders be present during *shivah*. In addition, it is of distinct value to have the family united during *shivah*.[10]

Of course, these days many families are scattered and it is not always possible for the entire family to be together. When the *shivah* house is far away from where a mourner lives, the mourner may return home for the last few days of *shivah* to give friends the opportunity to visit and offer their comfort and condolences. Many communities, especially those that attract transplants from other cities and countries, encourage mourners to have a "return *minyan*" for at least one night, even if the formal *shivah* period has ended.

A number of traditions are associated with the time immediately following a funeral. Neighbors, friends, and close relatives who are not principal mourners should be asked to make preparations at the *shivah* house. The mortuary will provide a seven-day memorial candle, which should be lit and placed in a public room. (See Chapter 8.) When there is more than one *shivah* house, each should have its own candle. Upon returning from the cemetery, it is customary to set out a pitcher of water and towels outside the house of mourning, so that people can wash before entering. This is a symbolic cleansing from going from a place associated with death to a place of life.

A mourner is forbidden to eat his or her own food at the first meal upon returning from the burial. Some explain that this is because sometimes the mourner refuses to eat and prefers death; thus, neighbors who cook for mourners are gently pushing them to accept the continuation of life.[11] And so it is that friends prepare the first full meal mourners eat after the funeral, a meal called the *seudat havra'ah* (meal of wellness). Usually the meal includes eggs, which are a symbol of life (one reason they are also found on the Seder plate). Eggs and other round foods (like lentils) are also served as a reminder of the Talmudic expression *"galgal chozer ba'olam"* (there is a recurring cycle in the world).

The elaborate meals that are frequently served at *shivah* houses today probably grew out of the tradition of the condolence meal. We must be mindful that this gathering is not a festive occasion. Excessive noise should be avoided, and the tone of conversations should be muted. Moreover, the mourner is specifically not obligated to entertain anyone. Even if friends are willing to do the work, we suggest that refreshments for visitors be kept to a minimum. Otherwise, one inevitably puts pressure on the mourner to play the host or hostess, which is inappropriate and unfair. Some congregations have even urged their members to eliminate the food service entirely since it can distort the *shivah* call into a different kind of social event.

The phrase "sitting *shivah*" comes from the practice of sitting on a stool or pillow at a lower level than normal. Some synagogues provide special *shivah* stools. In ancient days, mourners sat directly on the ground. This position can be understood as an enactment of the sense of being "pulled out" of life. Rabbi

Maurice Lamm explains it as, "almost in a literal sense, a physical adjustment to one's emotional state, a lowering of the body to the level of one's feelings, a symbolic enactment of remorse and desolation."[12] As further signs of mourning, many traditional Jews refrain from wearing leather shoes during *shivah*. It is also the custom to avoid non-essential grooming; men do not shave, and women generally avoid shaving their legs, tweezing their brows, wearing makeup, etc.

Many people are familiar with the practice of covering the mirrors in a house of mourning, and most probably consider it to be a superstitious holdover. When someone dies at home, the mirrors are covered so that the reflection of the body is not viewed. However, there is a good reason to cover mirrors in the *shivah* house regardless of where a person died. Remember, the mourner is supposed to have no social obligations during *shivah*, instead devoting one's time to grieving. Furthermore, people usually don't look their best when they are grieving. Covering the mirrors says, "Don't worry about your appearance. You have permission to look bereaved." It is another way of removing social pressure from the mourner. However, it is a custom, not a law.

SHABBAT, HOLY DAYS, AND THE END OF SHIVAH

Public mourning does not take place on Shabbat—although mourners are greeted specifically in *Kabbalat Shabbat*. The mourner is expected to attend synagogue services on Shabbat, and *shivah* continues after *Ma'ariv* (the evening service). In general, when one of the Three Pilgrimage Fesitvals (*Pesach*, *Shavuot*, and *Sukkot*), *Rosh Hashanah*, or *Yom Kippur* falls during *shivah* and *sh'loshim*, the observance of these holy days terminates observances of *shivah* and *sh'loshim*. Since these laws vary widely, it is best to consult your rabbi.

On the last day of *shivah*, we only sit for one hour in the morning. Afterwards, the mourners leave the home and take a walk around the block, symbolizing their re-entry into the world after a week spent at home. *In the Bond of Life*, The Rabbinical Assembly (Conservative) prayer book for a house of mourning, has a lovely service for concluding *shivah*. You may wish to recite a prayer like the one found in Chapter 8.

COMFORTING THE MOURNERS

During *shivah*, it is part of the *mitzvah* of *nichum aveilim* to visit the home of the mourner to bring comfort. People are sometimes reluctant to pay condolence calls. They worry about how they will be received and about what to say. They shouldn't worry. What is most important of all is simply your presence. A listening ear is more important than a golden tongue. Focus on the mourner and be guided by his or her mood, inclination to talk or be silent, and need to weep or laugh. Tradition wisely counsels us not to initiate conversation. Rather, one is to respond to the needs of the mourner and go with the conversation as the mourner determines it. It may very well be that at the moment of your visit, the mourner wishes to talk about something other than his or her grief. Let the mourner set the course. One cannot overly emphasize the wisdom of this teaching. So often, people avoid going to a house of mourning during *shivah* because they are afraid that they will do or say the wrong thing. Don't be afraid. If you live too far away to make a personal visit, you can still call, write a note, or make a donation in memory of the deceased. It is amazingly comforting to the mourners to be thought of and to have their loved ones and their loss be remembered.

Daily services, except for Shabbat, are usually conducted at the house of *shivah* to enable the mourners to say *Kaddish*. A word to mourners: People who wish to console you also come with their own emotional and experiential baggage. Yoel Ibn Shuaib, a Fifteenth-century rabbi, put it well, "All go to the house of mourning and each weeps over his own sorrow." You may well notice some people's uneasiness and emotional reactions. Or there may be people who say something stupid or cruel. Try to listen to the intention and not the words. It is unlikely that they intend to hurt you. Furthermore, you may find that you are suddenly very moved when certain people appear at the funeral, come to the house, write, call, or simply run into you by chance. Seeing that person may remind you once again of the reality of your loss. There is nothing you can do to avoid this, and it may comfort you to know that this happens to everyone, that such feelings recede with time, and that each encounter helps you become accustomed to and accept your loss.

AFTER SHIVAH

It is not easy to return to normal life immediately after the week of mourning. A degree of post-*shivah* letdown is hard to avoid. The house empties and people return to their normal routines, but the mourner realizes that the usual feels abnormal because of the void left by the death of a loved one. It is important for friends to realize that healing takes time. Stay in touch. A call two weeks, or a month after the funeral can often be very timely and helpful. For the mourner, the routine of coming to services to say *Kaddish* is also helpful.

Chapter 5
Sh'loshim and Beyond: Attaining Acceptance

SH'LOSHIM, THE FIRST YEAR, AND YAHRZEIT

After the end of *shivah*, there is a less intense mourning period known as *sh'loshim* (literally thirty), which lasts for thirty days counting from the day of the funeral. (So technically the first seven days of *sh'loshim* overlap *shivah*, and the less intense mourning continues for twenty-three days after *shivah* is over.) During *sh'loshim* the mourner returns to work but does not fully rejoin society. This separation is expressed by avoiding parties, concerts, and other forms of public entertainment. At the conclusion of the *sh'loshim*, mourning is over for all but those mourning their parents. For them, formal mourning lasts eleven months and includes the continual recitation of the *Kaddish*. Our synagogue often marks the end of *sh'loshim* by holding a special *minyan* during which mourners may speak or reminisce about the deceased or study together.

Judaism wisely insists that *Kaddish* can only be recited with a *minyan*. Forcing the mourners into the community to worship helps them to return to normal life, to accept the reality of their loss, and to understand that others have sustained similar losses and survived. The *Kaddish* tells us that we are not alone. In praising God, it suggests to us that no matter how sad we feel, we will learn to live and laugh again. Because remembrance plays such an important role, we observe the anniversary of death, *yahrzeit*, by lighting a candle in memory of the deceased and reciting *Kaddish* with the community. Congregations often send out yearly reminders of *yahrzeit* dates to mourners. The day itself is a kind of individual Memorial Day, a time to remember the deceased and reflect on his or importance in your life.

THE MONUMENT AND UNVEILING

The monument or grave marker can be selected shortly after the funeral, though we usually wait until after the eleventh month of mourning to have the unveiling. The full Hebrew name of the deceased as well as his or her English name should appear on the monument or plaque (some cemeteries do not allow upright monuments). Many people also include the Hebrew and English birth and death dates along with a short descriptive phrase. Your rabbi can help you select the text for a marker and fill out any associated paperwork.

The basic *mitzvah* involved in an unveiling is that of *kever avot* (visiting the grave), which can be done any time after the *sh'loshim* The unveiling is simply the first opportunity to visit the grave after the monument has been set in place. Customs differ, but usually the unveiling is timed to fall around the first *yahrzeit*.

The unveiling service is a relatively recent practice. It is very brief, usually consisting of some psalms and readings, a few words about the deceased, the removal of a covering from the tombstone, the *El Malei Rachamim*, and, if a *minyan* is present, the *Kaddish*. Suggested liturgies for men and women are included in Chapter 9. All three major movements within Judaism discourage the custom of bringing food to the cemetery to serve after the unveiling.

Some accuse the unveiling of re-opening old wounds, but it can also be understood as marking the end of formal mourning and the beginning of a new phase of life. The unveiling reminds us that while we will always remember the deceased—and always visit the grave on *yahrzeits* and during the Ten Days of Repentance—our own lives must continue.

TZEDAKAH

There is a close connection between *tzedakah* (charity) and various mourning customs. In the words of Rabbi Maurice Lamm, "Charity symbolizes the unity of all Israel. Contributions of time and effort and substance for the life of the community are an expression of unity. At the funeral it symbolizes the anguish felt in common by all Jews for the family of the deceased."[13] Thus, donations in memory of the deceased are more appropriate than flowers at a funeral. At a *yahrzeit*, it is customary to give *tzedakah* in memory of the deceased.

YIZKOR

Kaddish is also recited at *Yizkor* (memorial) services, which are held four times during the year: on *Yom Kippur*, on the eighth days of *Sukkot* and *Pesach*, and on the second day of *Shavuot*. *Yizkor* was originally instituted as a regular practice after the First Crusade in 1096, when entire communities of Jews in the Rhineland chose death over forced baptism. The surviving communities instituted a memorial service for these pious martyrs on *Yom Kippur*. Later, the memorial service was added to the other three holidays. And in an even later development, *Yizkor* services were understood to memorialize not only the Jewish martyrs, but also the departed relations of individual congregants. Often, congregations hold a brief service at the cemetery on the Sunday that precedes *Rosh Hashanah*.

Some may question the need to attend *Yizkor* services, and wonder why they should continue to grieve for their loved ones long after they have died. The simple answer is that *Yizkor*—as its Hebrew name implies—is about remembering, not grieving. Most of us, regardless of our belief in an afterlife, would agree with the notion that we live on in the memory of those who survive us. As such, we should recognize the value of ritualizing a moment of remembrance as an individual mourner and as part of the larger family of Jews.

Furthermore, we don't memorialize our loved ones simply by engaging our memory. Another, deeper tribute is to live life in accordance with their values and commitments. *Yizkor* is a time to reflect on and rediscover how we have absorbed and perpetuated the values of those we mourn.

Finally, we should not neglect *Yizkor*'s origins as a memorial for the martyrs of the Jewish people. *Yizkor* can become a moment of focused awareness of our place in the continuum of Jewish history, a silent meditation on how we can work to perpetuate the beliefs and commitments for which Jews have given up their lives. For all these reasons, we recommend that everyone participate in *Yizkor*, even those have no immediate family members to mourn. Everyone can benefit from memorializing our people's martyrs, and *Yizkor* can be a time of affirmation, even of thanksgiving to God, for the privilege of being a part of the Eternal People of Israel.

AFTERLIFE

The afterlife is a complicated and controversial topic, and one seldom discussed in American Jewish life. Many Jews are certain that Judaism does not believe in an afterlife. Yet one glance at the text of the *El Malei Rachamim* reveals that Judaism does indeed affirm the survival of the soul after death:

> "O God, full of compassion, eternal spirit of the universe, grant perfect rest under the wings of your presence to our loved one who has entered eternity. Let him/her find refuge forever in the shadow of your wings, and let his/her soul be bound up in the bond of eternal life. The Eternal God is his/her inheritance. May he/she rest in peace, and let us say: Amen."

We have deliberately quoted a Reform translation (from *Gates of the House*) to emphasize that belief in the afterlife is common to all three major branches of Judaism.

For many decades, the rationalistic bent of the modern movements, especially within the Conservative and Reform branches, made the afterlife a quasi-taboo topic. Now, in light of new attitudes and openness about the World to Come, we simply want to mention that it is certainly a viable Jewish option to believe in an afterlife. This belief doesn't diminish grief. After all, separation and loss are still an issue when a death occurs, even if we believe that the essence of each individual survives the body. But it can bring a measure of comfort.

Judaism has never codified a single picture of the afterlife, leaving us many options within the tradition. You may choose to believe, you may choose not to believe, you may choose to wait and see, but know that a belief in the afterlife is a part of Judaism.

Chapter 6
Guidelines for Grieving

In one of his many excellent books on death and mourning, Rabbi Earl Grollman lists ten guidelines for the mourner's process of moving "from helplessness to hopefulness." As you read through this list, which is based on interviews with many people who have suffered loss, you will see that we have added in brackets various practices we have discussed. Notice how *halachah* takes into account the human need for self-acceptance, emotional expression, support from others, time, and transcendence and how it mobilizes communal and personal resources to help us cope with our grief.

Accept your emotions.
Realize that grieving can be an emotional roller coaster, involving shock, guilt, denial, panic, anger, and even physical symptoms (*aninut* and its total suspension of social obligations, the staged mourning periods).

Express your feelings.
It is not enough to recognize your conflicting emotions; you must deal with them openly. A feeling that is denied expression is not destroyed; it remains with you and often erupts at inappropriate times. Acknowledging pain when you feel it is

much better for your long-term emotional health. You have a right to cry if you want to. It is a natural expression of grief for men as well as women and children (the pre-funeral eulogy discussion, *K'riah*, putting earth into the grave, saying *Kaddish*, sitting *shivah*).

Don't expect miracles overnight.
Heal in your own way and in your own time. Insist that others give you this freedom as well (rituals in Part II of this work, phased mourning periods).

Include children in the grieving process.
Children should not be shielded from tragedy. Silence and secrecy deprive them of an important opportunity to share grief. Your children's most important source of security is you. Stay close to them, hug them, and let them feel the warmth of your body (preparing for the eulogy, the funeral, *shivah*).

Don't isolate yourself.
If you stay alone too much, your home will become a protective shell that keeps you from facing the new challenges of life. At the same time, you should be careful not to overload your circuits by trying to do too much too soon. Early in your time of mourning, stick to what is important and necessary. Once you're ready to leave your house, take life one step and one task at a time (sitting *shivah* for a full week, the social aspects of *shivah*, taking a walk outside the house on the last day of *shivah*, going to services to say *Kaddish*, phased mourning periods).

Rely on your friends.
Let the right people know that you need support and feedback. Your friends cannot bring you comfort unless you allow them to share your sorrow (support during the period of *anin-*

ut, the funeral, *shivah*, help during the difficult days, weeks, or months after *shivah* has ended).

Help yourself and others through support groups.
People in these groups understand your fears and frustrations; they have been there before. The synagogue community, as indicated before, offers you a network of support (the funeral, *Kaddish*, *minyan*).

Consider counseling.
There is nothing wrong with obtaining help. There is everything wrong with suffering needless pain when assistance may be available. Getting professional advice is not an admission of weakness, but rather is a demonstration of determination to help yourself during this critical period.

Be nice to yourself.
You need people. You also need moments of solitude to find yourself. Your faith may also help you face and survive the inevitable moments of despair (all the rituals of mourning).

Try to turn your pain into a positive experience.
Death ends a life, not a relationship. Resolve to live as your beloved would want you to live, love as he or she would want you to love, and serve others as he or she would have wanted you to serve. Consider death a personal challenge to grow and better yourself (*yizkor*, *tzedakah*, naming a newborn child after the deceased, settling longstanding feuds and making peace within the family, returning slowly but steadily to life).[14]

SUMMARY

Our rabbis were wise in their understanding of human emotional needs, and the Jewish laws of mourning are a special gift borne of this wisdom. They give the bereaved a plan to follow, they provide structure during a time of turmoil, and they offer friends and family members guidance on how to help the bereaved.

Chapter 7
Checklist of Important Information

Most congregations issue a set of procedures to follow when a death occurs. Each year, when board and committee heads change, we at Congregation Netivot Shalom send an updated listing with phone numbers. Your congregation may want to do the same; following is a template.

1. Call the President, Vice President or *Chevra Kadisha* Coordinator. Members of the *Chevra Kadisha* are available to assist you with funeral arrangements and with information about cemeteries.

2. Call the rabbi. He or she will be able to help and advise in a number of ways.

3. Call a mortuary. The congregation will be able to help you select one.

4. Most congregations observe the traditional practices of a closed casket funeral and in-ground burial (no cremation). Other traditional practices your congregation may follow include *Taharah* (ritual washing), *tachrichim* (burial shrouds), and *sh'mirah* (accompanying the body until burial). Your rabbi and *Chevra Kadisha* members can explain your congregation's rules and procedures to you.

5. The mortuary staff will help you coordinate funeral arrangements with the cemetery. Check with the rabbi before finalizing the time for the funeral
6. Make sure that there are no problems with getting a death certificate. You or a member of your family needs to ensure that the doctor has signed the death certificate and that the certificate is available to the funeral home staff. You will need to order several official copies of the certified death certificate. The mortuary staff is experienced with these matters and can help and advise you.
7. Your call to an officer of the congregation or the rabbi can set in motion arrangements for a *minyan* at your home and notification of friends.
8. If burial is to take place out-of-town, the staff at the mortuary can help with those arrangements.
9. If you and the deceased live in different cities and the funeral will be held out of town, you should still notify your congregation and leave a phone number where you can be reached. You may also have questions about your return or need to make local arrangements. Plan to have a *minyan* here, even if *shivah* is officially over, so that your friends will have an opportunity to make a formal condolence call.

Part II

Compendium of Prayers

Chapter 8
Selection of Jewish Mourning Prayers

MOURNERS' KADDISH (to be recited with a *minyan*)

יִתְגַּדַּל וְיִתְקַדַּשׁ שְׁמֵהּ רַבָּא, בְּעָלְמָא דִּי בְרָא כִרְעוּתֵהּ, וְיַמְלִיךְ מַלְכוּתֵהּ, בְּחַיֵּיכוֹן וּבְיוֹמֵיכוֹן וּבְחַיֵּי דְכָל-בֵּית-יִשְׂרָאֵל, בַּעֲגָלָא וּבִזְמַן קָרִיב, וְאִמְרוּ: אָמֵן.

יְהֵא שְׁמֵהּ רַבָּא מְבָרַךְ לְעָלַם וּלְעָלְמֵי עָלְמַיָּא.

יִתְבָּרַךְ וְיִשְׁתַּבַּח וְיִתְפָּאַר וְיִתְרוֹמַם וְיִתְנַשֵּׂא, וְיִתְהַדָּר וְיִתְעַלֶּה וְיִתְהַלָּל שְׁמֵהּ דְּקֻדְשָׁא, בְּרִיךְ הוּא, לְעֵלָּא מִכָּל-בִּרְכָתָא וְשִׁירָתָא תֻּשְׁבְּחָתָא וְנֶחֱמָתָא דַּאֲמִירָן בְּעָלְמָא, וְאִמְרוּ: אָמֵן.

יְהֵא שְׁלָמָא רַבָּא מִן שְׁמַיָּא וְחַיִּים עָלֵינוּ וְעַל כָּל-יִשְׂרָאֵל, וְאִמְרוּ: אָמֵן.

עוֹשֶׂה שָׁלוֹם בִּמְרוֹמָיו, הוּא יַעֲשֶׂה שָׁלוֹם, עָלֵינוּ וְעַל כָּל-יִשְׂרָאֵל, וְאִמְרוּ: אָמֵן.

Yitgadal v'yitkadash sh'mei raba, b'alma di v'ra chirutei, v'yamlich malchutei, b'chayeichon uv'yomeichon uv'chayei d'chol-beit-yisrael, ba'agala uvizman kariv, v'imru: amen.

Y'hei sh'mei raba m'vorach l'olam ul'almei almaya.

Yitbarach v'yishtabach v'yitpa'ar v'yitromam v'yitnasei, v'yithadar v'yitaleh v'yithalal sh'mei d'kud'sha, b'rich hu, l'eila mikol birchata v'shirata, tushb'chata v'nechemata da'amiran b'alma, v'imru: amen.

Y'hei sh'lama raba min sh'maya v'chayim aleinu v'al kol-yisrael v'imru: amen.

Oseh shalom bim'romav hu ya'aseh shalom aleinu v'al kol-yisrael, v'imru: amen.

May God's great name be exalted and hallowed, as is God's wish, throughout the created world. And so may God's sovereignty soon be established, in your lifetime and in your days, and in the days of all the house of Israel; and respond with: Amen.

May God's great name be acknowledged forever and ever.

May the name of the Holy One, who is blessed, be acknowledged and celebrated, lauded and worshipped, exalted and honored, extolled and acclaimed, though God is truly far beyond all acknowledgement and praise, expressions of gratitude or consolation ever spoken in the world; and respond with: Amen.

May the prayers and pleas of all Israel be accepted by their Creator in the heaven; and respond with: Amen.

May abundant peace from heaven, and life, come to us and all Israel; and respond with: Amen.

May the One who brings harmony on high, bring harmony to us and to all Israel and respond with: Amen.

KADDISH AT A BURIAL (to be recited with a *minyan*)

יִתְגַּדַּל וְיִתְקַדַּשׁ שְׁמֵהּ רַבָּא, בְּעָלְמָא דִּי הוּא עָתִיד לְאִתְחַדָּתָא וּלְאַחֲיָאָה מֵתַיָּא וּלְאַסָּקָא יָתְהוֹן לְחַיֵּי עָלְמָא. וּלְמִבְנֵא קַרְתָּא דִּי יְרוּשְׁלֵם וּלְשַׁכְלָלָא הֵיכְלֵהּ בְּגַוַּהּ. וּלְמֶעְקַר פָּלְחָנָא נֻכְרָאָה מִן אַרְעָא וְלַאֲתָבָא פָּלְחָנָא דִּי שְׁמַיָּא לְאַתְרֵהּ. וְיַמְלִיךְ קֻדְשָׁא בְּרִיךְ הוּא בְּמַלְכוּתֵהּ וִיקָרֵהּ בְּחַיֵּיכוֹן וּבְיוֹמֵיכוֹן וּבְחַיֵּי דְכָל־בֵּית יִשְׂרָאֵל, בַּעֲגָלָא וּבִזְמַן קָרִיב, וְאִמְרוּ: אָמֵן.

יְהֵא שְׁמֵהּ רַבָּא מְבָרַךְ לְעָלַם וּלְעָלְמֵי עָלְמַיָּא.

יִתְבָּרַךְ וְיִשְׁתַּבַּח וְיִתְפָּאַר וְיִתְרוֹמַם וְיִתְנַשֵּׂא, וְיִתְהַדָּר וְיִתְעַלֶּה וְיִתְהַלָּל שְׁמֵהּ דְּקֻדְשָׁא, בְּרִיךְ הוּא, לְעֵלָּא מִכָּל־בִּרְכָתָא וְשִׁירָתָא תֻּשְׁבְּחָתָא וְנֶחֱמָתָא דַּאֲמִירָן בְּעָלְמָא, וְאִמְרוּ: אָמֵן.

יְהֵא שְׁלָמָא רַבָּא מִן שְׁמַיָּא, וְחַיִּים עָלֵינוּ וְעַל כָּל־יִשְׂרָאֵל, וְאִמְרוּ: אָמֵן.

עוֹשֶׂה שָׁלוֹם בִּמְרוֹמָיו, הוּא יַעֲשֶׂה שָׁלוֹם, עָלֵינוּ וְעַל כָּל־יִשְׂרָאֵל, וְאִמְרוּ: אָמֵן.

*Y*itgadal v'yitkadash sh'mei raba, b'alma di hu atid l'itchadata ul'achaya'ah meitaya ul'asaka yat'hon l'chayei alma. Ul'mivnei karta di yerush'leim ul'shach'lala heich'lei b'gavah. Ul'mekar pal'chana nuch'ra'ah min ara, v'la'atava pal'chana di sh'maya l'atrei. V'yamlich kud'sha b'rich hu. B'malchutei vikarei b'chayeichon uv'yomeichon uv'chayei d'chol-beit yisrael, ba'agala uviz'man kariv, v'imru: amen.

Y'hei sh'mei raba m'vorach l'olam ul'almei almaya.

Yitbarach v'yishtabach v'yitpa'ar v'yitromam v'yitnasei, v'yithadar v'yitaleh v'yithalal sh'mei d'kud'sha, b'rich hu. L'eila m' kol-birchata v'shirata, tushb'chata v'nechemata da'amiran b'alma, v'imru amen.

Y'hei sh'lama raba min sh'maya v'chayim aleinu v'al kol-yisrael v'imru: amen.

Oseh shalom bimromav hu ya'aseh shalom aleinu v'al kol-yisrael, v'imru: amen.

*M*ay God's great name be exalted and hallowed, as is God's wish throughout the world, which will be renewed. God will then restore the dead, raise them to eternal life, rebuild the city of Jerusalem, complete the Temple within it, uproot idolatry from the earth, and return our worship of God to the point where heaven and earth meet. And so may God's sovereignty soon be established, in your lifetime and in your days, and in the days of all the house of Israel; and respond with: Amen.

May God's great name be acknowledged forever and ever.

May the name of the Holy One, who is blessed, be acknowledged and celebrated, lauded and worshipped, exalted and honored, extolled and acclaimed, though God is truly far beyond all acknowledgement and praise, expressions of gratitude or consolation ever spoken in the world; and respond with: Amen.

May the prayers and pleas of all Israel be accepted by their Creator in heaven; and respond with: Amen.

May abundant peace from heaven, and life, come to us and all Israel; and respond with: Amen.

May the One who brings harmony on high, bring harmony to all Israel; and respond with: Amen.

EL MALEI RACHAMIM

El Malei Rachamim for a Woman

אֵל מָלֵא רַחֲמִים, שׁוֹכֵן בַּמְּרוֹמִים, הַמְצֵא מְנוּחָה נְכוֹנָה תַּחַת כַּנְפֵי הַשְּׁכִינָה, בְּמַעֲלוֹת קְדוֹשִׁים וּטְהוֹרִים כְּזֹהַר הָרָקִיעַ מַזְהִירִים, אֶת־נִשְׁמַת _____ בַּת _____ שֶׁהָלְכָה לְעוֹלָמָהּ, בְּגַן עֵדֶן תְּהֵא מְנוּחָתָהּ. אָנָּא, בַּעַל הָרַחֲמִים, הַסְתִּירֶהָ בְּסֵתֶר כְּנָפֶיךָ לְעוֹלָמִים, וּצְרוֹר בִּצְרוֹר הַחַיִּים אֶת־נִשְׁמָתָהּ, יהוה הוּא נַחֲלָתָהּ, וְתָנוּחַ בְּשָׁלוֹם עַל מִשְׁכָּבָהּ, וְנֹאמַר: אָמֵן.

El malei rachamim shochein bam'romim, hamtsei m'nucha n'chonah tachat kanfe hashchinah, b'ma'alot k'doshim ut'horim k'zohar harakiah mazhirim, et nishmat _____ bat _____ shehal'chah l'olamah, b'gan eiden t'hei m'nuchatah. Ana ba'al harachamim, hastireha b'seiter k'nafecha l'olamim, utsror bitsror hachayim et-nishmatah, Adonai hu nachalatah, v'tanuach b'shalom al mishcavah, v'nomar: amen.

El Malei Rachamim for a Man

אֵל מָלֵא רַחֲמִים, שׁוֹכֵן בַּמְּרוֹמִים, הַמְצֵא מְנוּחָה
נְכוֹנָה תַּחַת כַּנְפֵי הַשְּׁכִינָה, בְּמַעֲלוֹת קְדוֹשִׁים
וּטְהוֹרִים כְּזֹהַר הָרָקִיעַ מַזְהִירִים,
אֶת-נִשְׁמַת ‎_____‎ בֶּן ‎_____‎
שֶׁהָלַךְ לְעוֹלָמוֹ, בְּגַן עֵדֶן תְּהֵא מְנוּחָתוֹ.
אָנָּא, בַּעַל הָרַחֲמִים, הַסְתִּירֵהוּ בְּסֵתֶר כְּנָפֶיךָ
לְעוֹלָמִים, וּצְרוֹר בִּצְרוֹר הַחַיִּים אֶת-נִשְׁמָתוֹ,
יהוה הוּא נַחֲלָתוֹ, וְיָנוּחַ בְּשָׁלוֹם
עַל מִשְׁכָּבוֹ, וְנֹאמַר אָמֵן.

El malei rachamim shochein bam'romim, hamtsei m'nuchah n'chonah tachat kanfe hashchinah, b'ma'alot k'doshim ut'horim k'zohar harakiah mazhirim, et nishmat _____ ben _____ shehalach l'olamo, b'gan eiden t'hei m'nuchato. Ana ba'al harachamim, hastirehu b'seiter k'nafecha l'olamim, utsror bitsror hachayim et-nishmato, Adonai hu nachalato, v'yanuach b'shalom al mishcavo, v'nomar: amen.

For either male or female

Exalted, compassionate God, grant infinite rest, in your sheltering Presence, among the holy and pure, to the soul of _____, who has gone to (his/her) eternal home. Merciful One, we ask that our loved one find perfect peace in your eternal embrace. May (his/her) soul be bound up in the bond of life. May (he/she) rest in peace. And let us say: Amen.

LIGHTING THE SHIVAH CANDLE (option 1)

The light of life is a finite flame. Like the Shabbat candles, life is kindled. Like the Hanukkah candles, it is enough for one day, yet a beacon through the ages. It burns, it glows, it radiates warmth and beauty, and then it fades and is no more.

We must not despair. We are more than a memory vanishing in the darkness. With our lives we give life. With our light we illumine the darkness. something of us can never die; we move in the eternal cycle of darkness and death, of light and life.

As the shiva light burns pure and bright, so may the memory of our dear _____ brighten and purify our lives.

נֵר יהוה נִשְׁמַת אָדָם, חֹפֵשׂ כָּל חַדְרֵי־בָטֶן.

*N*eir Adonai nishmat adam, hofes kol hadrei vaten.

*T*he human spirit is the light of God, (a light) penetrating
one's most intimate being.
PROVERBS 20:27

שְׁמַע יִשְׂרָאֵל, יהוה אֱלֹהֵינוּ, יהוה אֶחָד.

*S*h'ma Yisrael, Adonai eloheinu, Adonai echad.

*H*ear, O Israel: Adonai is our God, Adonai is one.

Out of the depths we cry to you, Adonai. Hear our supplication. A heavy burden has fallen on our family and our community. We now turn to you, the source of goodness, for comfort and help. Give us the eyes to see that pain is not Your will, that somewhere, there weeps with us One who feels our trouble and knows the suffering of our souls. O Divine Spirit in whose image we are created, we seek the light to dispel the darkness that has overtaken us. Let us find You in the love of family and friends, in the sources of healing that are implanted within all the living, and in the mind that conquers all infirmity amid trouble. Grant us the courage to endure what cannot be escaped and the resolve to go on without bitterness or despair.

LIGHTING THE SHIVAH CANDLE (option 2)

נֵר יְיָ נִשְׁמַת אָדָם.

יְהִי רָצוֹן שֶׁתְּהֵא נִשְׁמַת ‎_____ (Insert Name)
צְרוּרָה בִּצְרוֹר הַחַיִּים עִם נִשְׁמַת אַבְרָהָם יִצְחָק יַעֲקֹב,
שָׂרָה רִבְקָה רָחֵל וְלֵאָה וְעִם נַפְשׁוֹת שְׁאָר
צַדִּיקִים וְצִדְקָנִיּוֹת בְּגַן עֵדֶן: אָמֵן.

Neir Adonai nishmat adam.

Y'hi ratson shet'hei nishmat _____ (insert name) ts'rura bitsror hachayim im nishmat Avraham, Yitschak, Ya'akov, Sarah, Rivkah, Rachel v'Leah v'im nafshot sh'ar tsadikim v'tsid'kaniyot b'gan eiden: Amen.

The human soul is a light from God.

May it be your will that the soul of _____ (insert name) enjoy eternal life, along with the souls of Abraham, Isaac, Jacob, Sarah, Rebecca, Rachel and Leah, and the rest of the righteous that are in the Garden of Eden: Amen.

CONCLUSION OF SHIVA (option 1)

כִּי לֹא לַקַּלִּים הַמֵּרוֹץ, וְלֹא לַגִּבּוֹרִים הַמִּלְחָמָה, וְגַם לֹא לַחֲכָמִים לֶחֶם, וְגַם לֹא לַנְּבֹנִים עֹשֶׁר וְגַם לֹא לַיֹּדְעִים חֵן, כִּי־עֵת וָפֶגַע יִקְרֶה אֶת־כֻּלָּם.

Ki lo lakalim hamerots, v'lo lagiborim hamilchamah, v'gam lo lachachamim lechem, v'gam lo lan'vonim osher v'gam lo layod'im chein, ki-eit vafega yik'reh et kulam.

The race is not won by the swift,
Nor the battle by the valiant,
Nor the bread won by the wise,
Nor wealth by the intelligent,
Nor favor by the learned.
For the time of mischance comes to all.
     ECCLESIASTES 9:11

הַזֹּרְעִים בְּדִמְעָה בְּרִנָּה יִקְצֹרוּ.

Hazorim b'dimah b'rinah yik'tsoru.

They who sow in tears shall reap with songs of joy.
     PSALM 126:5

Almighty God, healer of the brokenhearted, let neither death nor sorrow have dominion over us. Grant us comfort, strength, and consolation. May we always cherish what is imperishable in _____'s life. Bless us with love and with peace, that we serve you with all our heart. May _____'s memory inspire us to deeds of loving-kindness. Amen.

(After mourners rise, they take a short walk outside to symbolize their return to normal life.)

CONCLUSION OF SHIVA (option 2)

כְּאִישׁ אֲשֶׁר אִמּוֹ תְּנַחֲמֶנּוּ כֵּן אָנֹכִי אֲנַחֶמְכֶם וּבִירוּשָׁלַָם תְּנֻחָמוּ. לֹא־יָבוֹא עוֹד שִׁמְשֵׁךְ וִירֵחֵךְ לֹא יֵאָסֵף כִּי יְיָ יִהְיֶה־לָּךְ לְאוֹר עוֹלָם וְשָׁלְמוּ יְמֵי אֶבְלֵךְ. בִּלַּע הַמָּוֶת לָנֶצַח וּמָחָה יְיָ דִּמְעָה מֵעַל כָּל־פָּנִים.

K'ish asher imo t'nachmenu kein anochi anachem'chem uvirushalam t'nuchamu. Lo-yavo od shim'sheich vireiheich lo yei'aseif ki Adonai yih'yei-lach l'or olam v'shal'mu y'mei ev'leich. Bila hamavet lanetsach umachah Adonai dim'ah mei'al kol-panim.

As a mother comforts her children, so shall I comfort you, says Adonai. Your sun will set no more, neither will your moon be withdrawn. For Adonai will be your enduring light, and the days of your mourning will come to an end. God will wipe away tears from every face.

FROM ISAIAH 66:13, 60:20, 25:8

Almighty God, Master of Mercy, Healer of the broken-hearted, let neither death nor sorrow have dominion over us. Grant comfort, strength, and consolation to us. May we always cherish what is imperishable in the life of _____ Bless our family with love and with peace, that we may serve You with all our heart. May the memory of _____ inspire us to deeds of lovingkindness. And let us say: Amen

(After mourners rise, they take a short walk outside as a symbol of their return to normal life.)

LIGHTING A YAHRZEIT CANDLE

It Is Less Distant Now

The *yahrzeit* candle is different,
Announcing neither Sabbath nor Festival.
No benediction recited,
No song sung,
No psalm mandated.

Before this unlit candle,
Without a quorum, I stand,
Unstruck match in my hand.

It is less distant now,
the remembrance ritual of parents deceased.
I am older now,
closer to their age than before.
I am older now;
Their aches in my body
Their white hairs beneath my shaved skin
Their wrinkles creased into my face.

It is less distant now
This ritual
Once made me think of them
Now makes me think of me.
Once it recalled relationships to them
Now I ponder my children's relationship to me
Once I wonder what to remember of them
Now I ask what my children will remember of me
What smile, what grimace,
what stories they will tell their children?

It is less distant now.
How will I be remembered?
How will I be mourned?
Will they come to the synagogue,
Light a candle
Recite the *Kaddish*?
It is less distant now.

Once *yahrzeit* was about parents deceased
Now it is of children alive.
Once it was about a distant past
Now it is about tomorrow.

Rabbi Harold Schulweis

Chapter 9
Service for an Unveiling of a Marker

Choose from the following three readings:

Reading 1

יְיָ, מָה-אָדָם וַתֵּדָעֵהוּ, בֶּן-אֱנוֹשׁ וַתְּחַשְּׁבֵהוּ? אָדָם לַהֶבֶל דָּמָה; יָמָיו כְּצֵל עוֹבֵר. בַּבֹּקֶר יָצִיץ וְחָלָף, לָעֶרֶב יְמוֹלֵל וְיָבֵשׁ. תָּשֵׁב אֱנוֹשׁ עַד-דַּכָּא, וַתֹּאמֶר: "שׁוּבוּ, בְנֵי-אָדָם!" לוּ חָכְמוּ יַשְׂכִּילוּ זֹאת, יָבִינוּ לְאַחֲרִיתָם. כִּי לֹא בְמוֹתוֹ יִקַּח הַכֹּל; לֹא-יֵרֵד אַחֲרָיו כְּבוֹדוֹ. פֹּדֶה יְיָ נֶפֶשׁ עֲבָדָיו, וְלֹא יֶאְשְׁמוּ כָּל-הַחֹסִים בּוֹ.

Adonai mah adam vateida'eihu, ben-enosh vat'chash'vehu? Adam lahevel damah; yamav k'tseil over. Baboker yatsits v'chalaf, laerev y'moleil v'yaveish. Tasheiv enosh ad-daka, vatomer: "Shuvu, v'nei-adam!" Lu chach'mu yaskilu zot, yavinu l'acharitam. Ki lo v'moto yikach hakol; lo-yeireid acharav k'vodo. Podeh Adonai nefesh avadav, v'lo yesh'mu kol-hachosim bo.

God! What are we, that you have regard for us? What are we, that You are mindful of us? We are like a breath; our days are as a passing shadow; we come and go like grass that in the morning shoots up, renewed, and in the evening fades and withers. You cause us to revert to dust, saying: Return, O mortal creatures! Would that we were wise, that we understood where we are going! For when we die we carry nothing away; our glory does not accompany us. Mark the whole-hearted and behold the upright: they shall have peace, God. You redeem the soul of Your servants, and none who trust in You shall be desolate.

Reading 2

מִזְמוֹר לְדָוִד: יְהֹוָה רֹעִי לֹא אֶחְסָר:
בִּנְאוֹת דֶּשֶׁא יַרְבִּיצֵנִי, עַל־מֵי מְנֻחוֹת יְנַהֲלֵנִי:
נַפְשִׁי יְשׁוֹבֵב, יַנְחֵנִי בְמַעְגְּלֵי־צֶדֶק לְמַעַן שְׁמוֹ:
גַּם כִּי־אֵלֵךְ בְּגֵיא צַלְמָוֶת, לֹא־אִירָא רָע, כִּי־אַתָּה עִמָּדִי:
שִׁבְטְךָ וּמִשְׁעַנְתֶּךָ, הֵמָּה יְנַחֲמֻנִי:
תַּעֲרֹךְ לְפָנַי שֻׁלְחָן נֶגֶד צֹרְרָי, דִּשַּׁנְתָּ
בַשֶּׁמֶן רֹאשִׁי כּוֹסִי רְוָיָה:
אַךְ טוֹב וָחֶסֶד יִרְדְּפוּנִי כָּל־יְמֵי חַיָּי, וְשַׁבְתִּי
בְּבֵית־יְהֹוָה לְאֹרֶךְ יָמִים:

Mizmor l'David: Adonai ro'i lo echsar.
Binot deshe yarbitseini al-mei m'nuchot y'nahaleini.
Nafshi y'shoveiv, yancheini v'mag'lei-tsedek l'ma'an sh'mo.
Gam ki-eileich b'gei tsalmavet lo-ira ra, ki-atah imadi,
shiv't'cha umish'an'techa heimah y'nachamuni.
Ta'aroch l'fanai shulchan neged tsor'rai dishanta
vashemen roshi kosi r'vayah.
Ach tov vachesed yird'funi kol y'mei chaya, v'shavti b'veit-Adonai
l'orech yamim.

A Psalm of David

Adonai is my shepherd, I shall not want.
Giving me repose in green meadows,
Leading me beside the still waters
To revive my spirit,
Guiding me on the right path,
For that is God's essence.

Though I walk through the valley
Of the shadow of death,
I fear no harm, for You are with me.
Your staff and Your rod comfort me.

You prepare a banquet for me
In the presence of my foes.
You anoint my head with oil; my cup overflows.
Surely goodness and kindness
Shall be my portion all the days of my life.
And shall dwell in the
House of Adonai forever.

PSALM 23

Reading 3

שִׁיר לַמַּעֲלוֹת.
אֶשָּׂא עֵינַי אֶל-הֶהָרִים,
מֵאַיִן יָבֹא עֶזְרִי?
עֶזְרִי מֵעִם יְהוָה,
עֹשֵׂה שָׁמַיִם וָאָרֶץ.
אַל-יִתֵּן לַמּוֹט רַגְלֶךָ,
אַל-יָנוּם שֹׁמְרֶךָ.
הִנֵּה לֹא-יָנוּם וְלֹא יִישָׁן
שׁוֹמֵר יִשְׂרָאֵל.
יְהוָה שֹׁמְרֶךָ,
יְהוָה צִלְּךָ עַל-יַד יְמִינֶךָ.
יוֹמָם הַשֶּׁמֶשׁ לֹא-יַכֶּכָּה,
וְיָרֵחַ בַּלָּיְלָה.
יְהוָה יִשְׁמָרְךָ מִכָּל-רָע,
יִשְׁמֹר אֶת-נַפְשֶׁךָ.
יְהוָה יִשְׁמָר-צֵאתְךָ וּבוֹאֶךָ
מֵעַתָּה וְעַד-עוֹלָם.

Shir lama'alot.
Esa einai el-heharim,
mei'ayin yavo ezri.
Ezri me'im Adonai,
osei shamayim va'arets.
Al-yitein lamot raglecha,
al-yanum shom'recha.

Hinei lo-yanum v'lo yishan
shomeir Yisrael.
Adonai shom'recha
Adonai tsil'cha al-yad y'minecha.
Yomam hashemesh lo-yakekah,
v'yarei'ach balailah.
Adonai yishmar'cha mikol-ra,
yishmor et-nafshecha.
Adonai yishmar-tsei'cha uvo'echa
mei'atah v'ad-olam.

A Song for Ascents

I turn my eyes to the mountains;
from where will my help come?
My help comes from Adonai,
maker of heaven and earth.
God will not let your foot give way;
your guardian will not slumber.
Look, the guardian of Israel
neither slumbers nor sleeps!
Adonai is your protection,
a guardian at your right hand.
By day the sun will not strike you,
nor the moon by night.
Adonai will guard you from all harm;
God will guard your life.
Adonai guards your going and coming,
now and forever.

PSALM 121

READ TOGETHER

The Light of God

In Proverbs we read: "The human spirit is the light of God" (Proverbs 20:27). Within each of us, God implants a divine spark. Each of us has the obligation to tend this spark and fan it into a flame that will light up one's own life and the lives of others.

A lit candle can be snuffed out, or it can burn out, or it can kindle other candles. When the flame is passed on to others, the flame will continue to burn long after the original candle has been extinguished.

A thousand years, in the presence of the Eternal One, are but a day — the years of our life, a passing hour. Life has been given and life has been taken, and through it all we praise God's name.

We have been pained by the void created with _____'s passing. Yet love is strong as death. The bonds created by love are eternal. And ours is the blessing of memory, through which the lives of our departed continue to be with us.

In the name of _____'s family, and friends, we consecrate this monument, as an expression of our love and respect. (The cover is removed)

תְּהִי (נִשְׁמָתוֹ/נִשְׁמָתָהּ) צְרוּרָה בִּצְרוֹר הַחַיִּים.

T'hi (nishmato/nishmatah) ts'rurah bitsror hachayim.

*May (his/her) soul be bound up in the bond of life.
And let us all say: Amen.*

READ RESPONSIVELY

When We Remember Them
At the rising of the sun and at its going down
We remember them
>At the blowing of the wind
>and in the chill of winter
>We remember them.

At the opening of the buds and in the rebirth of spring
We remember them.
>At the blueness of the skies
>and in the warmth of summer
>We remember them.

At the rustling of the leaves and in the beauty of autumn
We remember them.
>At the beginning of the year and when it ends
>We remember them.

As long as we live, they too will live;
for they are now a part of us, as
We remember them.

> When we are weary and in need of strength
> We remember them.

When we are lost and sick at heart
We remember them.

> When we have joy we crave to share
> We remember them.

When we have decisions that are difficult ot make
We remember them.

> When we have achievements that are
> based on theirs,
> We remember them

As long as we live, they will live;
for they are now a part of us, as
We remember them.

> RABBI SYLVAN KAMENS AND RABBI JACK REIMER

If there is a *minyan*, conclude with Mourners' *Kaddish* on pages 46-47. If there is no *minyan*, conclude with *El Malei Rachamim* on pages 50-51.

Appendix 1
Glossary of Hebrew Terms

aninut The phase of mourning between death and burial

aron casket

aveil mourner

Baruch dayan ha'emet "Blessed is the true judge," traditional exclamation of acceptance upon hearing of someone's death

chesed shel emet "true loving kindness," refers to the care for the body of the deceased, since we can't expect anything in return

Chevra Kadisha Sacred or Holy Society, the group that prepares the body for burial and offers support services to mourners

El Malei Rachamim "God Full of Compassion," The memorial prayer that includes the name of the deceased and may be recited at any time

gemilut chasidim acts of kindness

halachah/halachic Jewish law/in accordance with Jewish law

hesped eulogy

kaddish prayer recited by a mourner

kever avot visiting the grave

k'riah tearing one's garment as a sign of mourning

k'vod hamet respect for the dead

l'vayah funeral (literally: accompanying)

matseivah gravestone, monument, or marker

minyan quorum of ten people required for praying as a community and reciting some prayers, including the *kaddish*

mitzvah commandment in Jewish law

nechamah comfort

nichum aveilim comforting of mourners

Olam habah The World to Come

onein person in a state of *aninut*

seudat havra'ah "meal of comfort" prepared by friends for the mourners to eat after the funeral

shivah seven-day period of mourning beginning with the day of burial

sh'loshim thirty day period of mourning (includes *shivah*) beginning on the day of burial

sh'mirah guard, watch

shomer guardian of the body before burial

tachrichim shrouds

Taharah "purification," the entire procedure of preparing bodies for burial and may also refer to one specific part of that process

tzedakah charity

vidui confession

yahrzeit annual anniversary of a person's death

yizkor memorial service recited in the synagogue on *Yom Kippur* and the last days of *Pesach*, *Shavuot* and *Sukkot*

Appendix 2
Notes

1. "The Psychological Wisdom of the Law," in Jack Riemer, ed., *Jewish Reflections on Death*, p. 97.
2. Isaac Klein, *A Guide to Jewish Religious Practice*, p. 278.
3. Maurice Lamm, *The Jewish Way in Death and Mourning*, p. 6.
4. Abraham Chill, *The Minagim*, p. 323.
5. Ibid, p. 97.
6. Lamm, p. 44.
7. Joel B. Wolowelsky, "Self-Confrontation and the Mourning Rituals," *Judaism*, Vol. 33, No.1 Winter 1984, p. 109.
8. "The Lord Was His," *Reflections On Death*, p. 54.
9. Shulchan Aruch, *Yoreh Deah*, chapter 394:1.
10. Lamm, Ibid.
11. Shulchan Aruch, *Orech Chaim*, chapter 378:1.
12. Lamm, p. 112.
13. Lamm, p. 76.
14. Abridged from *What Helped Me When My Loved One Died*.

Appendix 3
Bibliography and Suggestions for Further Reading

1. General Books on Death and Mourning

There is a vast literature—both general and Jewish—on the subject of death and bereavement. This is merely a partial list of the available material. Most of these books have bibliographies that will lead you further.

Angel, Marc. *The Orphaned Adult: Confronting the Death of a Parent.* New Jersey: Jason Aronson, 1997.

Brener, Anne. *Mourning and Mitzvah.* Woodstock, VT: Jewish Lights, 1993. A guided journal for walking the mourner's path through grief to healing.

Chiel, Samuel and Henry Dreher, *For Thou Art With Me: The Healing Power of Psalms.* Rodal, 2000.

Cohen, A., ed. *Job.* London: The Soncino Press, 1993.

Cutter, William, ed. *The Jewish Mourner's Handbook.* West Orange, NJ: Behrman House, Inc.

Davis, Avrahom, et al. *Hope and Prayer: A Collection of Psalms for Yahrzeit and in Times of Illness and Distress.* New York: KTAV, 1992.

Diamant, Anita. *Saying Kaddish.* New York: Schocken Books, 1998.

Geffen, Rela, ed. *Celebration and Renewal.* Philadelphia, PA: JPS, 1993. A review of all Jewish rites of passage.

Greenberg, Sidney. *A Treasury of Comfort.* Wilshire Book Company. An anthology of helpful readings from many literatures.

Grollman, Earl A. *Concerning Death: A Practical Guide for the Living.* Beacon Press, 1981. Includes advice on how to write a condolence letter, suggestions for how to talk to children about death, and a chapter on Jewish death and mourning rituals.

Grollman, Earl A. *Explaining Death to Children*. Beacon Press, 1967. A series of essays from various disciplines on the subject of children and death.

Harlow, Jules, ed. *The Bond of Life*. NY: The Rabbinical Assembly, 1983. The Bond of Life is a prayer book for the house of mourning that also contains essays, readings, and reflections to guide and comfort the mourner.

Isaacs, Ron H. and Olitzky Kerry, eds. *A Jewish Mourner's Handbook*. New York: KTAV, 1991.

Kelman, Stuart. *Chesed Shel Emet: The Truest Act of Kindness*. Albany, CA: EKS Publishing Company, 2000

Klein, Isaac. *A Guide to Jewish Religious Practice*. NY: The Jewish Theological Seminary of America, 1979. A very detailed guide to all aspects of Jewish ritual as prescribed by the Conservative movement.

Kramer, David. *The Meanings of Death in Rabbinic Judaism*. London: Routledge, 2000.

Lamm, Maurice. *The Jewish Way in Death and Mourning*. NY: Jonathan David, 1972. The standard Orthodox reference.

Mitchell, Stephen. *The Book of Job*. NY: Harper Perennial, 1987.

Nachmanides. *The Gate of Reward*, translated by Charles B. Chavel. New York: Shilo Publishing Company Inc., 1983.

Olitzky, Kerry. *Grief in Our Seasons: A Mourner's Kaddish Companion*. Woodstock, Vermont: Jewish Lights, 1998.

Orenstein, Debra. *Lifecycles*. Woodstock, VT: Jewish Lights, 1994. Women reflect on life passages and personal milestones.

Ozarowski, Joseph. *To Walk in God's Ways: Jewish Pastoral Perspective on Illness and Bereavement*. New York: Jason Aronson, 1995.

Pomerantz, B. *Bubby, Me, and Memories*. NY: Union of American Hebrew Congregations, 1982. Helps introduce children to loss and the power of memory.

Press, Chaim. *Concern for the Living: A Collection of Laws, Tradition, and Customs on Mourning, their Origin, and Rationale*. New York: Targum/Feldheim, 1990.

Rapoport, Nessa. *A Woman's Book of Grieving.* NY: William Morrow & Co., Inc., 1994. Through the solace of words and poetry, grief is first acknowledged and then healed. For women and men.

Reimer, Jack, ed. *Jewish Reflections on Death.* NY: Schocken Books, 1976.

Wrestling with the Angel: Jewish Insights on Death and Mourning. New York: Schocken, 1995.

Rozwaski, Chaim. *Jewish Meditations on the Meaning of Death.* New York: Jason Aronson, 1994.

Shapiro, Rami M. *Open Hands: A Jewish Guide on Dying, Death, and Bereavement.* Florida: Temple Beth Or, 1986.

Swirsky, Michael, ed. *At the Threshold: Jewish Meditations on Death.* New York: Jason Aronson, 1996.

Weintraub, Simkha, ed. *Healing of Soul, Healing of Body.* Woodstock, Vermont: Jewish Lights, 1994.

Weiss, Abner. *Death and Bereavement: A Halakhic Guide.* KTAV Publishing House, 1989.

Wieseltier, Leon. *Kaddish.* New York: Knopf, 1998

Wolfson, Ron. *A Time to Mourn; A Time to Comfort.* NY: Federation of Jewish Men's Clubs and University of Judaism, 1993.

2. The Afterlife

Gilman, Neil. *The Death of Death.* Woodstock, Vermont: Jewish Lights, 1997.

Raphael, Simcha Paul. *Jewish Veius of the Afterlife.* New York: Jason Aronson, 1996.

Solomon, Lewish D. *The Jewish book of Living and Dying.* New York: Jason Aronson, 1996.

Spitz, Elie Kaplan. *Does the Soul Survive?* New York: Jewish Lights, 2000.

Sonsino, Rifat and Daniel B. Syme. *What Happens After I Die?* New York: UAHC Press, 1990.